D1165235

Savvy

THAT FIGURES!

BY DANIELLE S. HAMMELEF

A CRASH COURSE IN *Math.*

CAPSTONE PRESS
a capstone imprint

Savvy Books are published by Capstone Press,
1710 Roe Crest Drive, North Mankato, Minnesota 56003
www.capstonepub.com

Library of Congress Cataloging-in-Publication Data
Hammelef, Danielle S. author.
  That figures! : a crash course in math / by Danielle Hammelef.
     pages cm.—(Savvy. Crash courses)
  Summary: "Simplifies middle school math curriculum and offers examples
and activities to show readers how the topics tie in to real life".
—Provided by publisher.
  Audience: Ages 9–12.
  Audience: Grades 4–6.
  Includes bibliographical references and index.
  ISBN 978-1-4914-0774-5 (library binding)
  ISBN 978-1-4914-0782-0 (paperback)
  ISBN 978-1-4914-0778-3 (ebook PDF)
1. Mathematics—Study and teaching (Middle school)—Juvenile
literature. I. Title.
  QA11.2.H35 2015
  510.71′2—dc23
                              2014007718

Editorial Credits
Editor: Jennifer Huston
Designer: Lori Bye
Media Researcher: Gina Kammer
Production Specialist: Kathy McColley

Capstone Press would like to thank Jeanette Horng for her help in development of this book.

Photo Credits
Dreamstime: Ndoeljindoel, 24 (left); iStockphotos: andresr, 56; Newscom: picture-alliance/dpa/
Uli Deck, 27 (left), KRT/GM, 27 (right); Shutterstock: AN NGUYEN (wrapping paper), 45, Artmim
(drum), 39, baibaz, 16, bejo (music notes), 12, 15, Bienchen-s (gift boxes), 45, Blend Images, 32,
Bombaert Patrick, 15, Brent Hofacker, 18, Chones (bills), 21, CREATISTA (smiling girl), 9, back cover,
crolique, 6, Dora Zett, 23, DVARG (tickets), 5, eleana, 43, Elena Schweitzer (potato), 24, elwynn,
31, Eric Isselee, 22, 26, Feng Yu (container), 47, Filip jorkman, 40, Filip Dokladal (graph), 51, fuyu
liu (bottle), 8, Godruma, 41, Gunnar Rathbun, 13, Ivonne Wierink, 7, Jenn Huls (ribbon), 17, JFunk
(cupcake), 51, jmcdermottillo (pop art style faces), cover and throughout, Karkas (sundress), 5,
KathyGold (Pi), 39, Kenneth Man, 36, Kesu, 49, Kudryashka, (hand drawn colorful wave pattern),
throughout, Liquid Works (circle design), 38, back cover, Madlen (cone), 47, maxstockphoto, 20,
mishabender (Pythagoras), 38, NatUlrich (girl reading), 29, Nik Merkulov, 30, Nikola Bilic, 50,
NinaM (lime), 8, NREY, 48, oksana2010 (popcorn), 17, Pupes, 19, Radoman Durkovic, 46, RusGri,
55, S. Miroff, 10, sergign, 33, STILLFX (coins), 21, Tad Denson, 52, Timothy Hodgkinson (spoons),
9, Toponium, 34, USBFCO (puzzle design), 11, Vitalinka, 28, Vixit (test), 29, weerapong pumpradit
(clocks), 12; SuperStock: Science Photo Library (girls blowing bubble gum), 11

Design elements: Shutterstock

Printed in the United States of America in Stevens Point, Wisconsin.
032014   008092WZF14

Table of Contents

HERE'S THE DEAL .... MATH IS FOR REAL.

Whether you realize it or not, you encounter math everywhere you go—not just at school. But in the real world, math doesn't lurk inside your teacher's desk, just waiting to quiz you.

Math helps you know what time you have to leave to meet your friends at the movies. It tells you if you can afford that cute sundress for vacation. Math also shows you how much to feed your new puppy.

Math Rules!

Can you think of a time when math is not around? People eat, sleep, play, and work with math every day—often without even knowing it. This Savvy girl's guide to math will take you step-by-step through some real-world exercises. For example, you'll learn how to figure out which sale on jeans gives you the best deal. You'll also learn to calculate how much money you'll need to earn over the summer to pay your cell phone bill for the entire year.

Just like learning to dance or play a sport takes time and hard work, training your brain does too. Remember, even if you don't get the answer on the first or second try, you are still getting smarter each time.

So grab some paper and a pencil and turn to the chapter of your choice. Then take a deep breath because you're about to experience aha moments and gain math savvy.

You may be thinking, "Do I have to read this book front to back?" Nope. You can turn to any section of any chapter to exercise your brain and sharpen those math skills.

CHAPTER 1

WHY FRACTIONS ARE A PIECE OF CAKE

Once you get the hang of them, fractions really are a piece of cake. OK, so that's not their technical definition—you can't exactly eat fractions. But when you eat a piece of cake, it's like you're eating a fraction because you're eating a part of a whole cake.

Go Figure!

Let's look at a tasty example. To celebrate your softball team's win in a tournament, you baked 24 yummy cupcakes.

But on the morning of the victory party, you discover that your brother and his friends ate 8 of your cupcakes! There's no time to bake more, but luckily you'll still have enough for everyone on the team.

Even so, you want to know what fraction of your original number of cupcakes you still have left. To get started, write the number of cupcakes you have left as the **numerator**. The number of cupcakes you started with is the **denominator**.

$$\frac{16}{24}$$ number of cupcakes left (24-8 = 16)

original number of cupcakes

We can reduce this fraction by using our **factoring** skills. First find the **greatest common factor (GCF)** of 16 and 24. Then divide both the numerator and denominator by the GCF. This will give us an equivalent fraction for ¹⁶/₂₄ in its simplest form.

Using your factoring know-how, you figure out that 8 goes into 16 and 24 equally without leaving any left over or remainder. In other words, the GCF for 16 and 24 is 8. So if we divide both the numerator and the denominator by 8, we get: $(16÷8)/(24÷8) = ^{2}/_{3}$

So you now have two-thirds the number of cupcakes that you originally had—thanks to your annoying brother and his friends.

MULTIPLYING FRACTIONS

You're probably wondering, "When will I ever need to multiply fractions?" Well, recipes often come with ingredients listed in fractions—1/2 cup, 1/4 teaspoon, 3/4 tablespoon, and so on. And sometimes you need to double or triple the recipe to make enough food. Multiplying fractions helps you get this information in a snap.

Go Figure!

Let's say you're making a marinade for a chicken dinner. Your recipe is for 4 servings, but tonight your family of 4 is hosting your cousin's family of 8. If the recipe calls for 1/2 cup of lime juice, 1/4 teaspoon of red pepper, and 2 1/2 cups of teriyaki sauce, how much of each ingredient do you need for your feast?

You'd better set a big table—you have 12 people coming to dinner, or 3 times as many as the recipe's serving size. This means that you'll need to multiply each ingredient by 3 to figure out how much you'll need for 12 people.

Let's start with the 1/2 cup of lime juice. To multiply fractions, you multiply the numerators together to get a new numerator, then you multiply the denominators together to get a new denominator. So your lime juice calculation looks like this:

$$1/2 \times 3 = ?$$

Wait a minute! This problem doesn't have two denominators. Now what?

Remember that any whole number can be written as an improper fraction with a denominator of 1, so $3 = 3/1$. So here's how your calculation looks as an improper fraction:

$1/2 \times 3/1 = (1 \times 3)/(2 \times 1) = 3/2$ cups of lime juice

To make measuring easier, let's change this into a **mixed number**:

$3/2$ cups $= 1 1/2$ cups

Now do the same for the other ingredients:

$1/4$ teaspoon of red pepper x $3/1 = (1 \times 3)/(4 \times 1) = 3/4$ teaspoon red pepper

$2 1/2$ cups of teriyaki sauce: (first change into an improper fraction): $5/2 \times 3/1 = (5 \times 3)/(2 \times 1) = 15/2$ cups $= 7 1/2$ cups of teriyaki sauce.

Now you're ready to mix up those ingredients and start cooking!

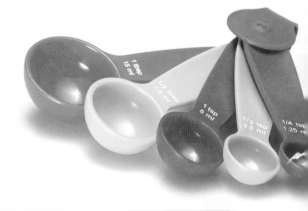

BE A MARVELOUS "MATHEMAGICIAN"!

Have a friend pick a whole number between 1 and 20 and keep it a secret. Ask her to double her number. Then tell her to add 6. Next, have her divide by 2. Ask her to tell you the quotient (the answer she calculated from dividing). Take the quotient and subtract 3. The difference is your friend's original number. Amaze your audience by announcing your friend's original number!

GOING TO PIECES: DIVIDING FRACTIONS

What's the inverse or opposite of multiplication? In other words, how would you "undo" multiplication? You got it: division! However, when you divide fractions, you end up multiplying the fractions. What??!! How can that be? This isn't a math trick or something that a math teacher made up long ago to confuse you. If we look at what's actually happening when you're dividing fractions, you can get a better idea of how this works.

Go Figure!

Let's say you want to have a bubble-blowing contest with your friends. You have a foot-long roll of bubble-gum tape. If each person needs $1\frac{1}{2}$ inches of gum to blow big bubbles, how many people can compete in your contest?

First write down your division problem, being careful to keep your units the same:

1 foot = 12 inches, so 12 inches of gum ÷ $1\frac{1}{2}$ inches per person = 12 inches of gum ÷ $\frac{3}{2}$ inches of gum per person.

It's really difficult to know how many $1\frac{1}{2}$-inch pieces will go evenly into 12 inches. So the trick is to change the division problem into a multiplication problem. Dividing by a fraction is the same as multiplying by its **reciprocal**.

To find the reciprocal of the second fraction, pull a "switcheroo" with the numerator and denominator. Then change the division sign to a multiplication sign. So now your problem looks like this:

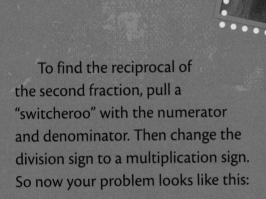

$$12 \div 3/2 = 12/1 \times 2/3 =$$
$$(12 \times 2)/(1 \times 3) = 24/3$$

Now reduce by dividing the numerator by the denominator: $24 \div 3 = 8$. You have enough gum for 8 people to blow bubbles in your contest.

Why can you just make a fraction "flip out?" Because multiplication and division do opposite jobs. (Whenever you divide by a number, it's the same as multiplying by its reciprocal.) After all, a fraction is really just a division problem in disguise.

Why couldn't the fraction make up its mind?

Because it was divided.

ADDING AND SUBTRACTING
FRACTIONS

Suppose you knew you only had so much time to get things done, how could you figure out if you could get it all done? Knowing how to add and subtract fractions will help you find the answers.

Go Figure!

Let's say your weekly flute practice log looks like this. How many total hours did you practice for the week?

	SUN.	MON.	TUES.	WED.	THURS.	FRI.	SAT.	Total:
Amount of time	1/2 hour	1 hour	1/4 hour	3/4 hour	1/2 hour	0 hour	1 1/2 hour	

When fractions have the same denominator (aka a common denominator), you can add or subtract them. Take $^1/_4$ and $^3/_4$, for example. To add these fractions together, you simply add the numerators together and keep their common denominators the same: $^1/_4 + ^3/_4 = (1 + 3)/4 = ^4/_4 = 1$.

Subtraction for these two fractions works the same way:

$^3/_4 - ^1/_4 = (3 - 1)/4 = ^2/_4$, which can be reduced to $^1/_2$.

But you can't add or subtract unlike fractions (fractions with different denominators), so you'll need to change them into like fractions. (If you have a mixed number, you must first change it into an improper fraction.)

To do that, you need to use your **least common multiple (LCM)** skills to find a common multiple for each denominator. Looking at the denominators in your flute practice log (2, 1, and 4), you know that the LCM is 4.

DATE	TIME (in hours)	Multiply by to get LCM in denominator	Equivalent fraction
SUNDAY	$1/2$	x $2/2$	$2/4$
MONDAY	$1/1$	x $4/4$	$4/4$
TUESDAY	$1/4$	x $1/1$ or no changes	$1/4$
WEDNESDAY	$3/4$	x $1/1$ or no changes	$3/4$
THURSDAY	$1/2$	x $2/2$	$2/4$
FRIDAY	0	x 0	0
SATURDAY	$1 1/2 = 3/2$	x $2/2$	$6/4$

Add up all the equivalent fractions to find your total time: $2/4 + 4/4 + 1/4 + 3/4 + 2/4 + 0 + 6/4 =$ $18/4$ hours. If you told your teacher you practiced $18/4$ hours, she would probably look at you as if you had two heads. So you need to change your improper fraction to a

mixed number before you write your total on your log: $18/4 = 4 2/4$ hours. We can reduce $2/4$ into its simplest form by dividing the numerator and denominator by a common factor. In this case, you can divide both by 2. Now your total time reads: $4 1/2$ hours.

What if your music teacher told the class that each week everyone should practice $5^3/4$ hours? (Where in the world did she come up with that figure?) How much more time do you need to practice to reach that goal?

For this problem, you need to figure out the difference between the total goal time ($5^3/4$ hours) and your actual total time ($4^1/2$ hours). Finding the difference means subtracting your time from the goal time. Since both numbers are mixed numbers, first change them into improper fractions. Before subtracting, we also need to turn them into like fractions:

$5^3/4 - 4^1/2 = {}^{23}/4 - {}^9/2$

(Multiply ${}^9/2$ by ${}^2/2$ to find the common denominator, which in this case is 4.)

So ${}^{23}/4 - {}^{18}/4 = {}^5/4 = 1^1/4$

You need to practice another $1^1/4$ hours. Looks like you shouldn't have skipped practice on Friday!

TRAIN YOUR BRAIN

Now it's your turn. Here are some real-life examples for you to solve using your knowledge of fractions.

1) You're going to a formal dinner/dance Saturday night. The dinner starts at 6 p.m., and it takes 30 minutes to get there. You want to get your hair styled and nails polished to match your dress. The salon is 15 minutes from your house. Your hair appointment will take $1\frac{1}{2}$ hours and your manicure will take 1 hour. If you want to make sure you have a half hour to get dressed, what is the latest you should make your salon appointment to arrive at the dinner/dance by 6 p.m.?

2) You're buying ribbon to make tricolor bracelets at a slumber party. You need $8\frac{1}{2}$ inches of each of the 3 colors of ribbon per bracelet. You have 11 guests coming to your party. How many total inches of ribbon should you buy? Don't forget to make a bracelet for yourself!

Answers on page 60.

3) You and your sister each make your own personal-sized pizzas. Your sister slices hers into 4 equal pieces. You slice yours into 6 equal pieces. If your sister eats 3 slices and you eat 4 slices, who has more leftovers?

Summing It Up

➤ In a fraction, the numerator is the number on top of the dividing line and the denominator is the number below it.

➤ Improper fractions and mixed numbers are two ways of writing fractions with values ≥ 1. Improper fractions have numerators ≥ their denominators. Mixed numbers are made up of an **integer** and a fraction.

➤ Before adding or subtracting fractions, the fractions must have common denominators. Then you add or subtract the numerators and keep the common denominator.

➤ To multiply fractions, you don't need common denominators. Instead, you simply multiply the numerators together to get a new numerator. Then you multiply the denominators together to get a new denominator.

➤ To divide fractions, you flip the second fraction upside down and then multiply the 2 fractions together.

➤ Equivalent fractions are fractions with the same value, such as $\frac{1}{2}$ and $\frac{2}{4}$.

CHAPTER 2

DECIMALS: THE TINY SECRET EVERY SAVVY SHOPPER KNOWS

You and your BFF decide to get smoothies on a hot summer day. Your friend orders a very-berry smoothie with whipped cream and a cherry on top. Her bill totals $3.98. You really want the same thing, but you only have $3. Instead you decide on a small mango-banana smoothie for $2.85, but then you remember you have to add 8% sales tax. Do you have enough money? Read on to find out.

If you know all about decimals—how to add, subtract, multiply, and divide them, as well as change them back and forth from fractions and percents—then shopping world, here you come! Oh, and that other world called math class, you'll be good to go there too.

Adding and Subtracting Decimals

At a neighbor's garage sale, you've found an AWESOME deal on a used skateboard. You also have your eye on a cute hot pink handbag and a sparkly bracelet. But you only have $10. Do you have enough for all three items? And if so, how much change should you get back? If you keep your decimals in order, money will make lots of "cents." LOL!

Go Figure!

Let's say the skateboard is marked $4.50, the handbag is $3.75, and the bracelet is 75 cents. First, let's find out if you have enough money for all three items.

Adding and subtracting numbers with decimals is just like adding and subtracting whole numbers, with one teeny-tiny difference: the decimal point. If you keep them lined up, you'll be all set to add and subtract.

all decimal points are aligned

↓

$4.50 (skateboard)
$3.75 (handbag)
+ $0.75 (bracelet)
──────────────
$9.00 (total for all three items)

Great! You have enough money for all three items. Now let's see how much change you should get back.

$10.00
- $ 9.00
──────────────
↓

$ 1.00

So you should receive $1.00 in change along with your cool new wheels, your hot new handbag, and your bling-tastic bracelet.

How did the decimal convince everyone it was right?

Everyone saw its point.

MULTIPLYING DECIMALS

When are you really going to need to know how to multiply decimals? Anytime you're dealing with dollars and cents. Want those cute shorts in all 5 colors? Want to know how much money you'll earn watering your neighbor's garden while she's on vacation? Knowing how to multiply decimals will help you keep track of your money.

Go Figure!

Let's say your parents have left $10 on the counter. They left a note asking you to buy 20 ears of sweet corn at the local farmer's market. When you get there, you notice the sign next to the pile of corn says 39¢ per ear. Do you have enough money to buy 20 ears?

QUICK TIP

Adding zeros to the right of the decimal point can change the number's value. If you add zeroes after the decimal point, make sure you add them all the way at the end. For example, adding a zero after the 4 in $10.40 doesn't change the number's value. But adding a zero before the 4 does: $10.04. When you compare these decimals, you see that $10.40 > $10.04.

Since you need to find the price of multiple ears of corn, you'll multiply the total number of ears you need by the price per ear. Then you can compare the total price with how much money is in your pocket.

Multiplying decimals is just like multiplying whole numbers. But before you begin, count the total number of digits to the right of the decimal points in both numbers. Then pretend the decimals aren't there at all and multiply the numbers together. Next, start at the right side of your product and move left. Count back the same number of places, and insert the decimal point.

Let's see how that works for your ears of corn:

20 x $0.39 ➝ count the total digits to the right of the decimal ➝2 digits

Now forget the decimal exists and multiply: 20 x 39 = 780

Now put the decimal point back in. Starting at the far right and moving left, count two place values and insert the decimal: $7.80. You'll need $7.80 to buy 20 ears of corn. Since you have a $10 bill, you have enough money. Did the note say you had to bring home the change?

DIVIDING DECIMALS

Long division might be taught differently in your school, but this is one way to tackle it.

Anytime you want to divide money up amongst your friends, you'll need to know how to handle that tiny decimal point. Calculating your batting average? You'll also need decimal division know-how.

Go Figure!

Let's say you and your sister fed the neighbor's 2 cats while he was away on business for 5 days. When he returned, he paid you $25. How do you split the pay equally?

When dividing decimals, keeping track of the decimal point is easiest when you write your division problem using the long division symbol. So your problem would look like this:

$2\overline{)25.00}$ ➤ the divisor here is 2 and 25.00 is the dividend.

Now bring the decimal point straight up through the "roof" of the long division symbol and continue dividing like a regular long division problem:

$$
\begin{array}{r}
12.50 \\
2\overline{)25.00} \\
\underline{-2} \\
5 \\
\underline{-4} \\
10 \\
\underline{-10} \\
0
\end{array}
$$
➤ this is the quotient

So you and your sister each earned $12.50.

22

Now let's say your neighbor's cats each needed extra vitamins once a day. Your neighbor explained that you need to measure 0.25 ounces of liquid vitamins and add it to each cat's food. If the bottle is brand new and holds 4.5 ounces, will you have enough for all 5 days for both cats?

Let's first figure out how long the 4.5-ounce bottle will last. First you'll need 0.25 ounces per day for 2 cats, which is 0.50 ounces per day. Then you'll need to divide 4.5 ounces by 0.50 ounces per day. But wait, how do you divide a number by a decimal?

Your division problem will start the same as before by setting up a long division problem:

$$0.5\overline{)4.5}$$

Wait! Where did the zero to the right of 0.5 go? Remember that zeros at the farthest right position in a decimal number only serve to mark place values.

Move the decimal point of the divisor enough spaces to the right to make it a whole number. Then move the decimal point in the dividend the same number of spaces. (Sometimes you may need to add zeros to the dividend in order to do this.)

$$5\overline{)45}$$ ➝ Here you moved the decimal point one space. Now divide normally:

$$5\overline{)45} \\ \begin{array}{r} 9 \\ -45 \\ \hline 0 \end{array}$$

Done! $4.5 \div 0.5 = 9$. The vitamin bottle will last 9 days, so you'll have enough!

CONVERTING DECIMALS TO FRACTIONS (AND BACK AGAIN)

As you know, fractions are really just undercover division problems. Pretty sneaky, huh? You write fractions as one number over another number separated by a dividing line. But you're probably wondering, "Outside of math class, when am I ever going to use this information?" Read on to find out.

Go Figure!

You're helping prepare your grandma's sweet potato casserole. Her recipe calls for 3½ cups of sweet potatoes. But you have 10-ounce cans of sweet potatoes. So how many ounces are in a cup? You find a cooking conversion chart that says 1 ounce = 0.125 cups. Great! You get out the measuring cups, but they're marked with fractions, not decimals. Now what? It's enough to make a girl's head spin. But not a math savvy girl like you!

As a fraction, 0.125 is written 125/1000. But there's no measuring cup in the world marked with this fraction, so you need to use your powers of reduction.

Remember if you divide both the top and bottom numbers by the same factor, you aren't changing the value of the fraction. You're just making equivalent fractions. Using your GCF skills, you see that the GCF for 125 and 1,000 is 125. Divide both numbers by 125, and the fraction $125/1000$ is reduced to $1/8$. So one ounce is equal to $1/8$ cup. Now you're cooking!

But how many cans do you need for your recipe? Each can is 10 ounces, so let's multiply 10 ounces by $1/8$ cup per ounce to find out how many cups there are in a can:

$10/1 \times 1/8 = 10/8 = 1^2/8 = 1^1/4$.

So there are 1¼ cups per can, but you need a total of 3½ cups. In order to calculate how many cans you need, you must figure out how many times 1¼ goes into 3½. To do this, divide 3½ by 1¼.

First change mixed numbers into improper fractions, so 3½ becomes $7/2$ and $1^1/4$ becomes $5/4$. Now divide:

$7/2 \div 5/4 = 7/2 \times 4/5 = 28/10 = 2^8/10$ cans.

Now let's convert our mixed number into a decimal. First change the mixed number back into an improper fraction, so $2^8/10$ becomes $28/10$. Divide 28 by 10 and voila! $2^8/10$ cans = 2.8 cans. Since you can't open exactly $8/10$ of a can, round up to the nearest whole can. You'll need to buy 3 cans of sweet potatoes for your recipe.

Math savvy girls know that fractions don't always have a denominator that's a multiple of 10, but we can still change it into a decimal. Say you find the perfect collar for your puppy. The collar costs $11 and is marked $1/3$ off. Before sales tax, how much will the collar cost?

Because the sale takes $1/3$ off the original price, that means you'll pay $2/3$ of the total price. Now let's figure out what $2/3$ of $11 is:

$$11 \times 2/3 = {}^{11}/_1 \times 2/3 = {}^{22}/_3$$

So before sales tax, you'll pay ${}^{\$22}/_3$. Cash or charge? Oh, wait. How much is that? Let's change the fraction into a decimal, so it looks like a dollar amount. Remember that fractions are division problems in disguise, so let's divide 22 by 3:

$$\begin{array}{r} 7.333 \\ 3\overline{)22.000} \\ -21\!\downarrow \\ \hline 10 \\ -9\!\downarrow \\ \hline 10 \\ -9\!\downarrow \\ \hline 10 \\ -9 \\ \hline 1 \end{array}$$

When will this division problem ever end? The answer—NEVER! This is a case of repeating decimals, and it's untreatable. The only thing you can do is make the decimal more comfortable by putting a little line over the repeating number, like this:

$7.3\overline{3}$

What does this mean for the cost of the collar? Since monetary values are written to the hundredths place, write two 3s after the decimal point and let it be. The collar will cost $7.33 before sales tax.

Math Savvy Women at Work

Heather Cooper, a development engineer for trucks at General Motors, is also a former sixth and eighth grade math teacher. Heather's job at General Motors is to make sure all the thousands of truck parts fit together to make a comfortable, safe, and appealing ride for the customer.

"As an engineer, I use math every day ... As a math teacher, I often saw kids trying to get an answer without really understanding what the numbers represented. It's important to know what the numbers mean so you get an answer that makes sense.

When I first started my engineering job, one thing that surprised me was my 'math problems' were missing key information. In school, your textbooks have all the information you need to find the answer to problems. Not in the real world. Here, I have to first figure out what information I need. Then I have to go and get that information to solve my problem. I ask questions and try to understand as much as I can before finding an answer."

PERCENTS

Maybe you don't realize it, but percents have been with you since the day you were born. Nurses measured your weight and height and then found your "percentage" on a growth chart. Percents stick with you all of your life—from test scores at school and sales at the mall to making money in business and at the bank. Percents are also used to measure an athlete's performance. Knowing how to deal with percents will not only make you math savvy, it will make you life savvy!

What Is a Percent?

Percent means "parts per hundred." So 50% off not only means a great sale on that cute bathing suit, but it also means you'd only pay $50 out of $100, or $^{50}/_{100}$ (which can be reduced to $^{1}/_{2}$), or "half off." Working with percents means knowing how to go back and forth between decimals and fractions.

Go Figure!

Let's say you scored 98% on your math test (woo-hoo!). If there were 50 questions, how many did you answer correctly? First you have to know what your test score tells you. A grade of 98% means you scored 98 out of 100 (or $^{98}/_{100}$) correctly. But since there weren't 100 questions, you'll need to convert the percent to a decimal. First drop the percent sign (%), and move the decimal to the left two places: 98% = 0.98. Why can you just move the decimal? Because you are technically dividing 98 by 100. This is just a super-quick shortcut.

Your quiz score was 9/10. Change that to a decimal, so 9 ÷ 10 = 0.9. To make this a percent, first move the decimal to the right two place values (now, you're technically multiplying by 100) and then add the % symbol. You scored 90%. So you scored better on your math test than on your science quiz, even though you only got one wrong answer on both. (Both are still AWESOME grades, BTW!)

So now you need to figure out how many questions you answered correctly out of 50. To do so, multiply the total number of test questions (50) by the decimal value (0.98):

50 x 0.98 = 49 correct out of 50 questions total. Well done!

Now suppose you also took a science quiz and scored 9 out of 10 correctly. Which did you do better on, the math test or the science quiz?

Time to work backward from the previous example and convert a decimal to a percent.

Why did the 2s stay away from the 3s?

The 2s thought the 3s were odd!

SALES TAX ALERT

Most businesses in the United States and Canada charge sales tax on things like shoes, cars, and computers. To calculate how much the sales tax will be, you first convert the percent into a decimal. For example, 6% = 0.06 and 8.25% = 0.0825. Then multiply the item's cost by the tax to get the amount to be added. So if you bought a bottle of purple plum nail polish for $3.00 and the sales tax is 7%, the tax will be: $3.00 x 0.07 = $0.21. So the final cost of the nail polish is: $3.00 + $0.21 = $3.21.

But there's a shortcut for finding an item's total price including sales tax. Because the sales tax is a percentage of the price, you can think of it as multiplying the cost by 1.00 plus the decimal form of the tax. So in this case: $3.00 x 1.07 = $3.21. Either way, we get the same final price for the nail polish!

Savvy Sale Shopping

Now let's get math savvy while shopping for a pair of jeans. A savvy shopper is never the victim of "sticker shock." Your favorite store is running a HUGE sale, and percents, decimals, and fractions are flying off the racks! You've narrowed your choices to three pairs of jeans and simply can't decide! But with only $30 in your wallet, which pair can you afford? Oh, and don't forget about the 7.25% sales tax.

The first pair is on sale for $28.50. With sales tax, the final sale price is $28.50 x 1.0725 = $30.56625, so we'll round that up to $30.57. Bummer! That's more money than you have in your wallet. Put those back and move on to the next pair!

The next pair is marked 30% off the original price of $40. So the sale price is 100% − 30% = 70% of the original price. First change the percent into a decimal: 70% = 0.70. Then multiply the original price by the decimal form: $40 x 0.70 = $28. With tax, you'll have to pay: $28 x 1.0725 = $30.03. SO close! Next!

The final pair of jeans is $34 and ¼ off. You can deal directly with the fraction and multiply it by the original price, but we like decimals better, so let's change the ¼ to its equivalent decimal, 0.25.

The discount is $34 x 0.25 = $8.50. So before tax, the sale price is $34 − $8.50 = $25.50. Will this pair bust your wallet too? Add the sales tax: $25.50 x 1.0725 = $27.35! That leaves you with $30 − $27.35 = $2.65 to spare. Whew! It pays to be math savvy!

A Math Savvy Guide to Equivalent Percents, Decimals, and Fractions

Some percents, decimals, and fractions appear almost every day in real life. Committing their equivalents to memory will help you make quicker calculations and leave more time for shopping!

Percent	Decimal Equivalent	Fraction Equivalent
12.5%	0.125	1/8
25%	0.25	1/4
33%	0.33	1/3
50%	0.5	1/2
75%	0.75	3/4

TRAIN YOUR BRAIN

1) You and 5 friends just finished eating lunch at a restaurant and the waitress (who was super-friendly) brings your bill. The total bill is $29.94 but she forgot to add the 8% sales tax. Great service means your waitress deserves a great tip. If you want to add a 20% tip to the total, how much would you each pay, including tax and tip? (FYI, math-savvy tippers know to calculate tips on the total bill before taxes.)

2) You need 12 colored pencils for an art project. The art store sells pencils in packs of 12 for $10, packs of 6 for $7, and single pencils for $1.30. Which is the best deal? If you only needed 4 colors, which deal should you take to spend the least?

3) You want to buy a book for vacation. You found the perfect one for $8.99. You have a 5% off coupon and a $0.50 off coupon but can only use one deal. Which would save you more money?

Answers on page 60.

Summing It Up

➤ When adding and subtracting decimals, make sure you line up the decimal points before finding the sum or difference.

➤ Multiplying decimals is just like regular everyday multiplication, except you must first count the total number of digits to the right of the decimal point in each number. Then add the decimal point to the product by counting the same total number of digits from right to left.

➤ When dividing decimals, first move the divisor's decimal point enough places to the right to make it a whole number. Then put the decimal point on top of the long division bar before dividing. Move the decimal point of the dividend to the right the same number of places before dividing.

➤ To change a decimal into a fraction, the digits to the right of the decimal point are the numerator. The denominator is the place value of the last digit.

➤ When changing a percent to a decimal, drop the percent sign and move the decimal point two places to the left. Move the decimal point two places to the right when going from a decimal to a percent.

➤ To convert a percent into a fraction, make the "percent" number the numerator over a denominator of 100. To make a fraction into a percent, first convert the fraction into a decimal then change the decimal into a percent.

CHAPTER 3

IT'S AS EASY AS PI

Look around—everything you see—your house, your school books, the planet Earth—is made of shapes, lines, curves, and angles. Geometry is a branch of mathematics that helps you understand how your world shapes up. You may not even realize that you are already using geometry when you draw or when you're choosing a new home for your pet fish. So let's find out why shaping up with geometry is as easy as pi.

Plane Shapes

Two-dimensional shapes that you can draw on a piece of paper—such as triangles, squares, and circles—are plane shapes. They have a length and width but no thickness.

Plane shapes that have all straight sides are called **polygons**. Polygons got their names by the number of sides they have.

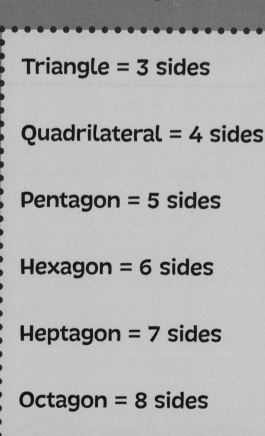

Triangle = 3 sides

Quadrilateral = 4 sides

Pentagon = 5 sides

Hexagon = 6 sides

Heptagon = 7 sides

Octagon = 8 sides

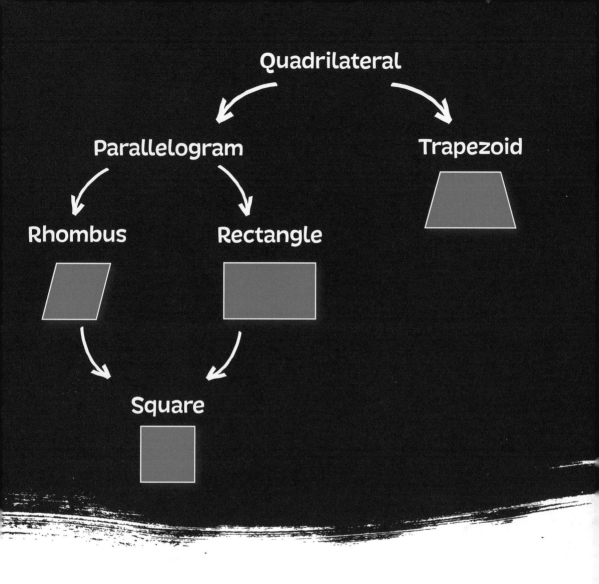

The Quadrilateral Family Tree: Just One "Branch" of Geome"tree"

Quadrilaterals are a group of polygons that have four sides. Rectangles, squares, rhombuses, and trapezoids are all quadrilaterals. Trapezoids have one pair of opposite sides that are **parallel**. In a parallelogram, both pairs of opposite sides are parallel. A rhombus is a special type of parallelogram.

In a rhombus, both pairs of opposite sides are parallel and all four sides have equal lengths. Rectangles are also parallelograms, but all of their sides meet at right angles. Squares have features from both the rhombus and the rectangle—all four sides meet at right angles and are of equal lengths.

PERIMETER

Ever hear of a security guard or soldier "walking the perimeter?" That means she's checking out the boundary or edges of the property. The perimeter of a shape is the distance along the edge of it. For polygons, you just add the lengths of all the sides to find their perimeters. For circles, you'll need to know an ancient secret. More on that later.

Go Figure!

Let's say your track coach wants everyone to run 2 miles at least 3 times a week. You live on a rectangular city block that's 600 feet long and 300 feet wide. How many times do you need to run around the block to travel 2 miles?

Let's start by drawing a diagram of your block:

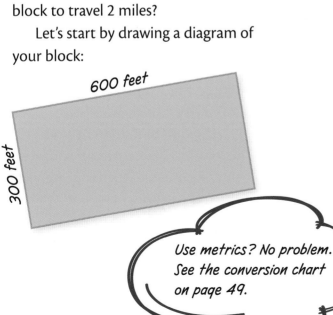

600 feet

300 feet

Use metrics? No problem. See the conversion chart on page 49.

To find the perimeter of polygons, you just add the sides:
600 feet + 600 feet + 300 feet + 300 feet = 1,800 feet. So once around the block totals 1,800 feet.

How many times do you need to run around the block to complete 2 miles? First you need to know how to change feet into miles. A distance conversion chart shows that 1 mile = 5,280 feet. Let's convert 1,800 feet into miles and see how close once around the block gets you:

5,280 feet ÷ 1,800 feet ≈ 0.34 miles

Since you're decimal and percent savvy, you know that 0.34 miles is 34%. Your powers of estimation tell you that you need to run the perimeter of your block about 3 times to equal 1 mile and 6 times for 2 miles. Let's do the math:

1,800 feet x 6 = 10,800 feet ➝ 10,800 feet ÷ 5,280 feet ≈ 2 miles.

Now lace up your shoes and hit the ground running. And don't forget to count how many times you pass your house!

The Many Sides and Angles of Triangles

Triangles all have 3 sides and 3 angles, but there are many different types depending on the lengths of their sides and the size of their angles:

Type of Triangle	Description
Equilateral	All sides are equal in length
Isosceles	Two of the three sides are equal in length
Scalene	No sides are of equal length
Right	Has one right angle (90°)
Acute	Each angle measures less than 90°
Obtuse	Has one angle measuring between 90° and 180°

CIRCLES

Pssst ... Here's that ancient secret we mentioned earlier: 3.14159 ... It's a never-ending constant value that every circle has in common.

About 2,200 years ago, a Greek mathematician named Archimedes proved that the **circumference** of a circle divided by its **diameter** is always the exact same number! And for every circle—no matter how big or small—that number is about 3.14. This constant is called pi, which sounds just like the pie you can eat. (And pies are circular. What a coincidence!)

About 300 years ago, people started using the Greek letter for "p" to represent pi. That symbol looks like this: π. However, the numbers 3.14 are only the first few digits of pi. The digits continue FOREVER without repeating. OMG!

Ἀρχιμήδης
Archimedes

Go Figure!

Let's say that you play the snare drum in the marching band. For an upcoming concert, you want to decorate the circumference of your drum with paper fringe in your school colors. If your drum is 12 inches in diameter, how long should the piece of fringe be? Let's find out.

The length of fringe will be equal to the circumference (C) of the drum. We know from Archimedes' ancient secret that circumference divided by diameter equals π. For your drum: C ÷ 12 inches = π, so C ÷ 12 ≈ 3.14

Because we have to find the value of the circumference, we have to get it by itself on one side of the equation. We can rewrite this equation as a fraction: C ÷ 12 ≈ 3.14 is the same as C/12 ≈ 3.14

Now we can multiply both sides by 12 to find the circumference: 12 x C/12 ≈ 3.14 x 12. The 12s cancel each other out (or equal 1) on the left side, leaving C alone: C ≈ 37.68 inches. If we round up to the nearest whole number, 38 inches of fringe should "circle" your drum. Drumroll please!

CELEBRATE PI

What are you doing next March 14? How about celebrating Pi Day! Since 1988, people have been celebrating all things "pi" on 3/14. Besides eating pie, having pie-eating contests, making pizza pies, and parading with pie plates, some celebrations hire skywriting pilots to write π in the sky!

AREA

You may not yet know what your "area of expertise" is, but you can find the area of polygons and circles. And who knows? Perhaps math will be your area of expertise!

Go Figure!

Your friend Grace has to make Papua New Guinea's flag for International Day at school. But Grace can't thread a needle, let alone sew, so she's asked you to help her since you are "the most talented seamstress" she knows. You're also the only person Grace knows with a sewing machine, but that's beside the point.

Here's a photo with the dimensions of the flag. Grace says she can scan the bird and stars images and cut those out. But how much red and black fabric does she need to buy? Her flag will hang on a wall, so she'll also need a plain white fabric backing.

The first thing you notice is that the flag is a rectangle cut into 2 right triangles. Let's start with the rectangle that makes up the white backing. You can find the area of a rectangle by multiplying the length (L) by the height (H). For the white fabric backing, the length is 36 inches and the height is 24 inches, so: Area (A) = 36 inches x 24 inches = 864 in² of white material.

24 inches

36 inches

Notice that our units are in inches squared (in^2). Whenever you measure area—whether you're measuring inches, feet, meters, or miles—those units will be squared. For instance, the area of a bedroom that's 14 feet x 16 feet would be 224 square feet (aka 224 sq. ft. or 224 ft^2).

Now for the triangles. Triangles are simply rectangles cut in half, so the area of a triangle uses the formula: $A = \frac{1}{2}(L \times H)$.

Both the black and the red triangles are equal in size, so you only need to find the area of one triangle and multiply it by 2 (it pays to be math savvy!).

$A = \frac{1}{2} \times 36$ inches x 24 inches = 432 in^2 of black fabric AND 432 in^2 of red fabric!

If we check our work, we see that the area of the two triangles equals the area of the white rectangular backing. Grace will need 864 in^2 of white fabric backing and 432 in^2 each of red and black fabric for her (or rather your) flag project.

AREA OF CIRCLES

Remember how circles have that ancient secret (pi) that's related to circumference and diameter? Well, pi can also help you find a circle's area, using the formula:

A = π x r² where r = the circle's **radius**.

Go Figure!

Let's take the π secret to the pizza parlor! The Pizza in a Pinch menu has three sizes of pizzas based on their diameters: a small (10-inch) costs $10, a medium (15-inch) costs $15, and a large (18-inch) costs $18. When you order a large, the clerk tells you they're running a special on the small pizzas—two for $16. "It's like getting 20 inches of pizza for less money than the 18-inch!" he says. That sounds like a good deal, but is he right? To find out, let's compare the areas.

To find the area of the pizzas, first we need to figure out the radius for each size. Remember that the radius is equal to ¹/₂ the diameter, so r = d/2. For the large pizza, r = ¹⁸/₂, so r = 9. For the small pizza r = ¹⁰/₂, so r = 5. Now let's get back to finding the area for each pizza.

Area of one large pizza =
πr² = π(9)² = π(81) ≈ 254 in²

Area of two small pizzas =
2 x πr² = 2π(5)² = 2π(25) ≈ 157 in²

JUST JOKIN'

Who am I? I am an odd number, but I become even if you take away one letter.

So the large pizza gives you a lot more square inches of pizza (i.e., more pizza to eat!), but which deal gives you the most pizza for your money? To find out, we need to figure out the price per square inch of both deals. The large pizza costs $18 for about 254 in^2, so price per in^2 = $18/(254 in^2) $\approx$ $0.07 per in^2.

The price for two small pizzas per in^2 = $16/157 in^2 $\approx$ $0.10 per in^2. That's 3 cents MORE per square inch than the large. So the clerk was wrong! The large pizza gives you the best value for your money. Apparently the clerk just isn't math savvy like you!

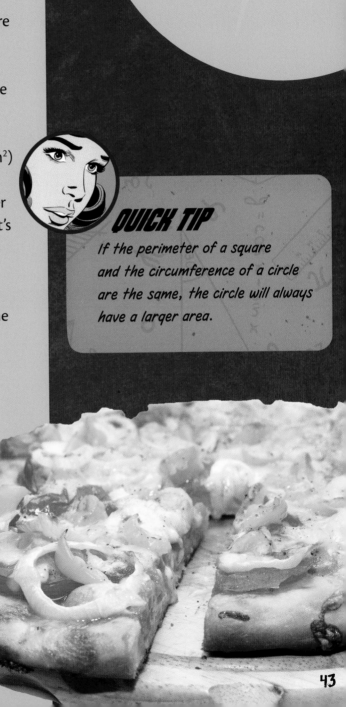

QUICK TIP

If the perimeter of a square and the circumference of a circle are the same, the circle will always have a larger area.

SURFACE AREA OF SOLIDS

Wrapping gifts is fun—and challenging too when you have odd shapes like a bottle or a cone. And you can't wait to see the look on your friend's face when she opens the birthday present you got for her. But did you know that when you wrap the package in paper, you're covering the **surface area** of the container?

Gift boxes come in many different three-dimensional (3-D) shapes. The most common gift box is in the shape of a rectangular **prism**, like a shoe box or a shirt box.

Go Figure!

You've purchased a mani/pedi set for your friend's birthday gift. You decide to wrap it in a shoe box that's 12 inches long by 4 inches wide by 5 inches high.

How much wrapping paper will you need to completely cover the shoe box with none left over?

The amount of wrapping paper needed is the same as the surface area of the box, which in this case is a rectangular prism. You know the formula for finding the area of a rectangle is A = L x H. You can find the total surface area by adding together the areas of all 6 faces of the box.

Let's start with the 2 ends of the box—the sides with the smallest dimensions:
A = 4 inches x 5 inches = 20 in².
And you have 2 ends to wrap, so multiply your area by 2:
20 in² x 2 = 40 in².

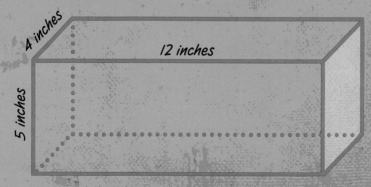

4 inches

12 inches

5 inches

Next, let's consider the top and bottom faces which are 12 inches long by 4 inches wide: A = 12 inches x 4 inches = 48 in². Again you're wrapping 2 faces with the same dimensions, so 48 in² x 2 = 96 in².

The last faces are 12 inches long by 5 inches high. Finding the area: A = 12 inches x 5 inches = 60 in² x 2 faces = 120 in².

How much wrapping paper do you need? Add all the individual areas together to find the surface area of the box: 40 in² + 96 in² + 120 in² = 256 in² of wrapping paper. Your friend is going to LOVE her gift!

TURN UP THE VOLUME!

All 3-D objects have **volume**. Volume is the amount of stuff you can put inside a 3-D object. Different 3-D objects have different formulas for finding their volumes.

Go Figure!

Let's say you're turning your old sandbox into a garden. Your sandbox is a rectangular prism with a base of 8 feet by 10 feet. You want to know how much soil you'll need to buy to make sure you have soil measuring 9 inches deep. But before you can plug the sandbox's height into the formula, you have to make sure you are working in the same units. Right now, we're dealing with feet and inches. So let's first change inches into feet: 9 inches x (1 foot)/(12 inches) = (9 feet)/12 = 0.75 feet

> *The inches cancel each other out.*

Now let's get back to finding the volume of the soil needed. According to the chart below, V = L x W x H, so V = 8 feet x 10 feet x 0.75 feet = 60 cubic feet (ft³). Fresh veggies, here we come!

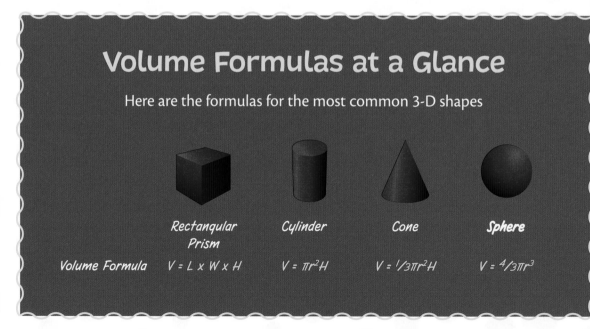

Volume Formulas at a Glance

Here are the formulas for the most common 3-D shapes

	Rectangular Prism	Cylinder	Cone	Sphere
Volume Formula	V = L x W x H	V = πr²H	V = ¹/₃πr²H	V = ⁴/₃πr³

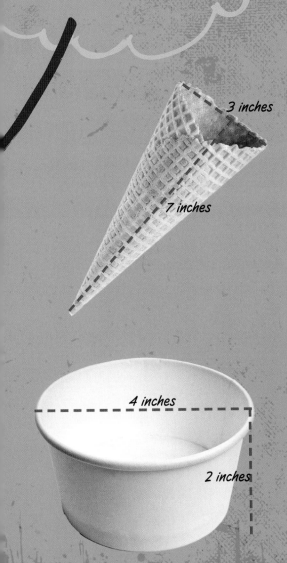

Just as area is measured in square units, volume is measured in cubic units. So in this example, we were using feet, so our volume is calculated in cubic feet (or ft³).

3 inches

7 inches

4 inches

2 inches

Go Figure!

Whew! Building a garden is hard work! You decide you want to cool off with ice cream. But would you get more ice cream in a cone measuring 7 inches high with a diameter of 3 inches or a cylindrical dish measuring 2 inches high with a diameter of 4 inches?

You know the diameters of the cylinder and the top face of the cone, so divide both diameters by 2 to find the radius of each.

radius of cone = 1$\frac{1}{2}$ inches

radius of cylinder = 2 inches

Now plug those into the formulas shown in the handy-dandy chart.

V of cone = $\frac{1}{3}$ π (1$\frac{1}{2}$ in)^2 x 7 in ≈ 16.5 in^3

V of cylinder = π (2 in)^2 x 2 in ≈ 25.1 in^3

So if you use the dish, you'll get to eat 1$\frac{1}{2}$ times as much ice cream ... assuming you don't heap it over the top of the cone or dish. Yummy!

TRAIN YOUR BRAIN

1) It's time to repaint your room. Good-bye boring off-white walls, hello gecko green! You measure your bedroom and find you have a square room with 12-foot-wide walls and an 8-foot-high ceiling. If a gallon of paint covers 350 square feet, and you need 2 coats of paint, how many gallons of paint do you need?

2) You are wrapping gifts for disadvantaged children. You have 20 gifts, each in a shoe box measuring 10 inches long by 6 inches wide by 4 inches high. If wrapping paper comes in rolls of 750 square inches, how many rolls will you need to buy, assuming you can use all of it with no waste?

Answers on page 60.

Summing It Up

➡ Polygons are straight-sided plane shapes that are named after the number of sides they have.

➡ The perimeter of a shape is the distance along the edge of it.

➡ Pi (π) is equal to ≈ 3.14159, and it's a constant for every circle.

➡ Area is the amount of flat space inside the boundaries of a polygon or circle.

➡ Surface area is the sum of all the areas of the faces of a 3-D object.

➡ Volume is the amount of stuff you can put inside a 3-D object.

3) You're getting 3 pet goldfish and need to buy a tank. You need 5 gallons of water per goldfish. The pet store has a cylindrical tank that's 18 inches high with a radius of 8 inches. The store also has a rectangular tank in stock that measures 16 inches long by 12 inches wide by 13 inches high. Which tank would be best for your new pets? (Note: 1 in³ = 0.004329 gallons) What if you can only afford the smaller tank? How many fish should you get?

Go Metric

It's easy to change measurements to metric! Just use this chart.

To Change	into	multiply by
inches	centimeters	2.54
inches	millimeters	25.4
feet	meters	.305
yards	meters	.914
gallons	liters	3.7854

CHAPTER 4

PLOTTING YOUR NEXT MOVE

You have a ton of data from your science project. How can you show your data in an easy-to-understand way? Maybe you want to know when you can afford those cute boots at the mall. What can you use to show your savings trend?

Powerful math tools such as graphs, charts, and plots will save the day! These organized pictures of your data make it easier and faster to show people what the data means.

Setting the Bar High with Bar Charts

Bar charts make it easy to show relative sizes at a glance. They are used to compare things between different groups or to track large changes over time.

Let's say you're in charge of ordering a sweet treat for a school dance. You narrow it down to 4 choices and decide to take a survey to find out how many people prefer each treat. How can you best organize that information and show it to others in an easy-to-understand way? Using a bar chart, of course!

Go Figure!

Here are the results from your sweet treat survey: 40 people love cupcakes, 25 prefer cookies, 20 like pudding cups best, and 15 opt for the "healthful" snack of apples with caramel sauce.

For your bar chart, you have 4 categories to compare, so you'll have 4 rectangular bars. The length of each bar will equal the total number of votes for each treat. You can draw the bars horizontally (across) or vertically (up and down), it's your choice. Using graph paper will help you draw your bars.

Let's go with a vertical bar chart. Starting with the horizontal **axis** labeled "Type of Treat," write your categories across the page along this axis, leaving equal space between each. Then draw a vertical axis labeled with what you counted: "Number of Students."

Now build your columns by counting up along the vertical axis. (Because our numbers go up so high, label the lines in increments of 10.) Starting with cupcakes, shade up to the line for 40 going up vertically from the horizontal axis. Do the same for the other 3 treats.

With your bar chart, it's easy to see that more students prefer cupcakes than the other 3 choices. You probably can't go wrong serving cookies though. But apple slices with caramel are the least favorite treat.

Bar Chart Drawing Tips

• For vertical bar charts, the vertical axis should start at zero and only go as high as your highest value. (So if the highest value is 12, don't number to 50). For horizontal bar charts, you number the horizontal axis.

• Label the numbers on the lines, not in the spaces.

• Space the numbers evenly (number by 1s, 2s, 5s, 10s, and so on) to fill up the page. No need to squeeze your chart into one corner of your graph paper.

• For vertical bar charts, draw the bars up from the horizontal axis, making each bar the same width. For horizontal bar charts, draw the bars out from the vertical axis.

• Space the bars evenly, giving them their personal space.

• Label what each bar represents.

• Have fun and color or shade each bar differently.

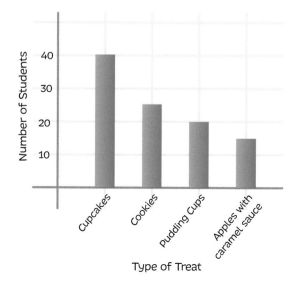

LINE CHART: A BAR CHART WITHOUT THE BARS

Line charts track changes over time. When smaller changes exist, line charts are better to use than bar charts. You can even use line charts to compare changes over the same period of time for more than one category—like comparing your rate of growth to your friend's.

Line charts are really just vertical bar charts without bars. Instead of bars, they use points. Line charts are built in a similar way to bar charts. The horizontal axis represents the **independent variable**, such as time.

The vertical axis shows the **dependent variable**, which is the quantity of the category or categories you're measuring.

Go Figure!

Let's say you've been working on your volleyball serve. You want to find out if you're improving, so you ask your coach for your serve record. Because you are tracking your progress over time and the changes are small, a line chart will work best. Here is your serve record:

Match	1	2	3	4	5	6	7	8	9	10	11	12
Good Serves	5	6	8	3	10	9	8	12	11	9	10	10
Bad Serves	3	2	4	6	1	2	2	4	1	0	1	0

To build your line chart, grab a piece of graph paper and draw and label your axes. The horizontal axis will be the volleyball season shown as "matches." The vertical axis will be the number of serves.

Now you're ready to plot your data points. Let's start with Match 1 and the number of good serves (5).

Find 5 along the vertical axis and Match 1 on the horizontal axis. Draw a symbol, such as a dot or square, at the spot where those two items **intersect** on the chart. Keep plotting the good serves for all 12 matches using the same symbol and same color for each. Then connect the symbols (in order) with straight lines.

Now do the same for the bad serves. Because you are tracking both good and bad serves, make the line colors and symbols different so you can easily tell them apart.

Finally, add a legend that shows what the different colored lines and symbols represent. The legend should include small "samples" of what the plot points look like for both your good serves and bad serves.

So what does your line chart tell you at a glance? Looking at your serving progress, ideally you'd want a larger difference between the good and bad serves. In other words, you want the lines to open up wide like an alligator's mouth as the season progresses. You also want the line representing your good serves to stay above your bad serves. You don't want the lines to touch or—even worse—cross each other!

So your chart tells you that overall, your serving improved over the season. You had one big setback in Match 4. (Yikes! The lines crossed!) But that's normal as you try new things to improve yourself.

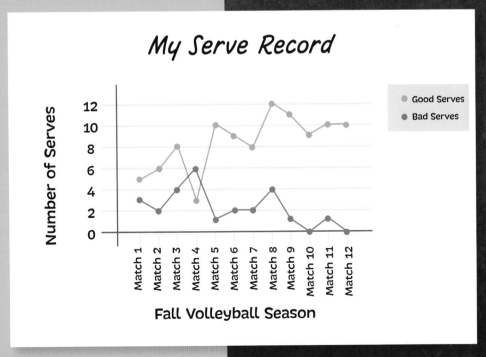

HOW BIG IS YOUR SLICE OF THE PIE?

When you need to compare parts of a whole, such as how much time of your day you spend at different activities or on what things you spend your money, pie charts are your best graphing choice. Pie charts do not show changes over time. That's where bar charts and line charts take the stage. Instead, pie charts show percentages of the total in each category.

Pie charts use "slices" to show relative sizes of data at a glance (or percentages of a whole). As an added bonus, you can choose to make each "slice of pie" a different color, making them an eye-catching accessory to any report.

Go Figure!

Let's say you want to start taking singing lessons on Monday evenings, but you've been told that your schedule is already "way too packed on Mondays."

You really want to learn to sing and know you have room in your day for lessons. How can you best show what you already know?

Because you want to compare parts of a whole, you can use a pie chart. The chart is the "whole" (your after-school time) and the "slices" are the segments or chunks of time spent doing certain activities.

First you'll need to keep track of how you spend your time after school and how long you spend doing each activity. BTW, your alarm blasts your favorite tunes at 6 a.m. sharp and your bedtime of 9 p.m. is nonnegotiable. Here are your activities for Mondays after school gets out at 3 p.m.:

Activity	Amount of Time
Homework	1.5 hours
Watch TV	1 hour
Basketball Practice	2 hours
Dinner	0.5 hour
Texting/e-mail/Computer	1 hour

The next step is to add up all your times to find the total:

1.5 + 1 + 2 + 0.5 + 1 = 6 hours

Notice that every hour, minute, and second of your after-school time is accounted for—from the moment the school bell rings until you plop into bed. Next turn each value into a percentage by dividing each value by the total.

Activity	Amount of Time	Percentage of the Whole (rounded to the nearest whole number)
Homework	1.5 hours	25%
Watch TV	1 hour	17%
Basketball Practice	2 hours	33%
Dinner	0.5 hour	8%
Texting/e-mail/Computer	1 hour	17%

Using percentages won't give you the exact number of degrees for each slice, so you'll need to round to the nearest whole number. You could also convert each amount of time into a fraction of the whole, which will give you a more precise measurement when converting to degrees.

Check to make sure your percentages add up to 100%:

25% + 17% + 33% + 8% + 17% = 100%

JUST JOKIN'

Why did the line chart make a bad lion cage at the zoo?

Answer: Because it had no bars.

Now it's time to draw your pie chart. You'll need a ruler, a compass, and a protractor. First draw a circle using your compass. Then use the ruler to draw a line segment from the circle's center to the edge of the circle at the 12 o'clock position. This radius will be the left-side edge of your first piece of pie.

Next you need to size your pieces of pie by finding out how many degrees are in each portion. A circle has 360 degrees (°). So to find out how many degrees each category represents, multiply each percentage by 360°. (Round to the nearest whole number that's divisible by 5.)

Homework: .25 x 360 degrees = 90 degrees
TV: .17 x 360 degrees = 60 degrees
Basketball: .33 x 360 degrees = 120 degrees
Dinner: .08 x 360 degrees = 30 degrees
Texting/e-mail/computer: .17 x 360 degrees = 60 degrees

Check your work by adding all your degrees to make sure you have a whole circle:

$$90° + 60° + 120° + 30° + 60° = 360°$$

Now measure your categories in terms of degrees on your circle. First place the zero-line of the protractor at the 12 o'clock position. Then moving clockwise, measure 90°. Moving clockwise from there, measure 60°. Always start at the place where you left off, so you continue going around the circle. Then continue measuring 120°, 30°, and 60°. You should end up back at your 12 o'clock starting point.

Next color each of your slices with a different color. Label each "slice" with its percentage and category (or add a legend box to your chart). And finally, give your chart a title.

Your chart clearly shows that basketball takes up most of your time on Mondays. And since homework and dinner are also nonnegotiable (like bedtime), you have to decide if you can give up all or some of your TV and texting/e-mailing/computer time to squeeze in a one-hour singing lesson. (Perhaps you can record your TV shows and text while your mom drives you to your lesson.) Are you full of pie charts yet?

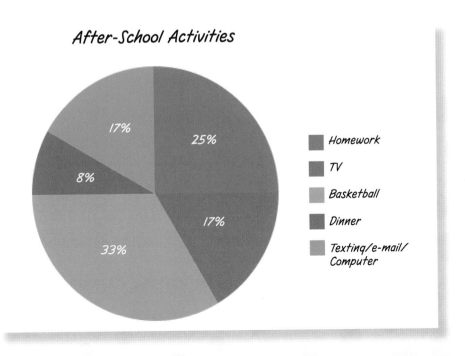

After-School Activities

- 17%
- 25%
- 8%
- 17%
- 33%

Legend:
- Homework
- TV
- Basketball
- Dinner
- Texting/e-mail/Computer

TRAIN YOUR BRAIN

1) You and your friend have started two blogs—one reviewing TV shows and one reviewing video games. You post once a week on both blogs, but you've decided to cut back to just one blog. Before you choose which blog to cut, you want to know more information about your readers. You've collected your traffic data for the past week and graphed the number of hits for each day using the line graph below.

a) What day(s) of the week did your blogs get the most views? How about the least hits?

b) Which blog is more popular— TV or video games?

2) Let's say your class of 40 students voted on fabric colors for class T-shirts. Draw a pie chart in your notebook that represents the following survey results:

green: 2 students; red: 4 students; purple: 8 students; black: 10 students; blue: 16 students.

Month	April	May	June	July	Aug.	Sept.	Oct.	Nov. – March
Income	80	40	120	90	70	100	50	0

3) You need to save money to pay a monthly cell phone bill of $50. To earn money, you walk your neighbors' dog while they are at work or on vacation. If you earn the monthly totals shown, will you have enough income to pay your cell bill for the entire year?

Answers on page 61.

Summing It Up

➤ Bar charts are used to compare things between different groups or to track large changes over time. They can be drawn with horizontal or vertical bars. Your choice!

➤ A line chart is a graph that uses points connected by lines to show how something changes in value over time.

➤ A pie chart is a circular chart divided into "slices," where each slice shows the size of each part compared to the whole.

Wrapping It Up

Math is everywhere—at the mall, in your kitchen, on your shampoo bottle—not to mention in your school. And since you eat, breathe, play, and sleep math every day, math can be one of your BFFs. How? By becoming math savvy and understanding what all the numbers around you mean and how to deal with them. You'll know if you're getting a good deal at the mall, how much flour to use in a recipe, and if your athletic performance is improving. You'll save time and money. You'll make healthier food choices. You'll gain a deeper understanding of science, music, and history. Now isn't that the kind of friend you want to hang out with? Math rules!

TRAIN YOUR BRAIN
ANSWER KEY

Chapter 1

1) 2:15 p.m.

2) You need 306 inches of ribbon to make 12 bracelets (don't 4get to make 1 for yourself!)

3) You have more pizza left over. You have ⅓ of a pizza left over and your sister has ¼.

Chapter 2

1) A 20% tip on $29.94 = $5.99. 8% sales tax on $29.94 = $2.40. Adding tip and sales tax to the original total = $29.94 + $5.99 + $2.40 = $38.33. Divide that by six people ($38.33 ÷ 6 = $6.39), so each person pays $6.39 including the tax and tip.

2) The best deal is 12 for $10. If you only need 4 pencils, you'd spend less money buying the singles.

3) The $0.50 coupon saves the most money.

Chapter 3

1) You need to buy 3 gallons of paint. Two gallons would cover 700 square feet, but you will need to cover 768 square feet in order to apply 2 coats.

2) You will need to buy 7 rolls of wrapping paper.

3) You need 15 gallons, so buy the cylindrical tank. If you bought the rectangular tank, you could only get 2 fish.

Chapter 4

1) a) On Saturday both blogs had the most views. The TV show blog had the least number of views on Tuesday and the video-game blog had the least views on Sunday.

b) The TV show blog is more popular than the video-game blog.

2) Your pie chart should look like this:

T-shirt Colors

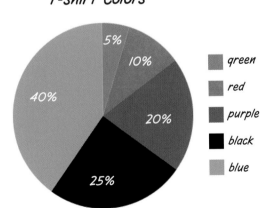

3) You made $550 for the seven months you walked the dog, which averages out to $45.83 per month over the course of 12 months, which is $4.17 short per month. Another way to look at it is that you needed to make $600 per year (12 months x $50 per month), and you only made $550. Either way, you come up short.

GLOSSARY

axis (AK-siss)—a line at the side or the bottom of a graph

circumference (sur-KUHM-fur-uhnss)—the length of the outer edge of a circle

denominator (di-NOM-uh-nay-tur)—the bottom number in a fraction that shows how many equal parts the whole number can be divided into

dependent variable (dee-PEN-duhnt VAIR-ee-uh-buhl)—the quantity of the category or categories being measured, which in a line graph is the vertical axis; its value depends on the independent variable.

diameter (dye-AM-uh-tur)—the length of a straight line segment through the center of a circle

factor (FAK-tur)—a whole number that can be divided evenly into a larger number with no remainder; to reduce a whole number by dividing it evenly by another number with no remainder

greatest common factor (GCF) (GRAYT-ist KOM-uhn FAK-tur)—the largest number that two or more numbers can all be divided by without leaving any left over or a remainder

independent variable (in-di-PEN-duhnt VAIR-ee-uh-buhl)—the part of an experiment or equation that changes; in a line graph it is represented by the horizontal axis

integer (IN-tuh-jur)—the whole numbers and their opposites, e.g., −2, −1, 0, 1, 2

intersect (in-tur-SEKT)—to meet or cross at one or more points; two or more things coming together

least common multiple (LCM) (LEEST KOM-uhn MUHL-tuh-puhl)—the smallest number that is a multiple of each of two or more numbers

mixed number (MIKSSD NUHM-bur)—a number made up of an integer and a fraction, such as $6\frac{1}{2}$

numerator (NOO-mer-ray-tur)—the top number in a fraction that shows how many equal parts of the denominator are being counted

parallel (PA-ruh-lel)—always the same distance apart and never touching

polygon (POL-ee-gon)—a flat, closed figure with three or more sides

prism (PRIZ-uhm)—an object with two opposite ends that are parallel polygons and faces that are each parallelograms

radius (RAY-dee-uhss)—a straight line segment drawn from the center of a circle to its outer edge

reciprocal (ree-SIP-ruh-kuhl)—the opposite or inverse of a fraction, which when multiplied by the original fraction has a product of 1

sphere (SFIHR)—a solid, round shape like a basketball or globe

surface area (SUR-fiss AIR-ee-uh)—the sum of all the areas of the faces of a 3-D object

volume (VOL-yuhm)—the amount of space taken up by an object or substance

READ MORE

Brunner-Jass, Renata. *Designer Digs: Finding Area and Surface Area.* iMath. Chicago, Norwood House Press, 2013.

Robinson, Tom. *Soccer: Math on the Field.* Math in Sports. Mankato, Minn., Child's World, 2013.

Somervill, Barbara A. *Distance, Area, and Volume.* Measure It! Chicago: Heinemann, 2011.

Wingard-Nelson, Rebecca. *Decimals and Fractions: It's Easy.* Easy Genius Math. Berkeley Heights, N.J.: Enslow Publishers, 2014.

INTERNET SITES

FactHound offers a safe, fun way to find Internet sites related to this book. All of the sites on FactHound have been researched by our staff.

Here's all you do:

Visit www.facthound.com

Type in this code: 9781491407745

Super-cool stuff!

Check out projects, games and lots more at
www.capstonekids.com

INDEX